BEARS/ LOS OSOS

by JoAnn Early Macken

Reading consultant: Susan Nations, M.Ed., author/literacy coach/consultant

WEEKLY WR READER®
EARLY LEARNING LIBRARY

Please visit our web site at: www.garethstevens.com
For a free color catalog describing our list of high-quality books,
call 1-800-542-2595 (USA) or 1-800-387-3178 (Canada).

Library of Congress Cataloging-in-Publication Data available upon request from publisher.
Fax (414) 336-0157 for the attention of the Publishing Records Department.

ISBN-10: 0-8368-3998-6 (lib. bdg.)
ISBN-13: 978-0-8368-3998-2 (lib. bdg.)
ISBN-10: 0-8368-4003-8 (softcover)
ISBN-13: 978-0-8368-4003-2 (softcover)

This edition first published in 2004 by
Weekly Reader® Books
An imprint of Gareth Stevens Publishing
1 Reader's Digest Road
Pleasantville, NY 10570-7000 USA

Copyright © 2004 by Weekly Reader® Early Learning Library

Art direction: Tammy West
Production: Beth Meinholz
Photo research: Diane Laska-Swanke
Graphic design: Katherine A. Goedheer
Translation: Colleen Coffey and Consuelo Carrillo

Photo credits: Cover © Lynne Ledbettor/Visuals Unlimited; title, pp. 13, 17, 21 © James P. Rowan;
p. 5 © Diane Laska-Swanke; pp. 7, 15 © Joe McDonald/Visuals Unlimited; p. 9 © Greg W. Lasley/KAC
Productions; p. 11 © Fritz Pölking/Visuals Unlimited; p. 19 © Gerard Fuehrer/Visuals Unlimited

Printed in the United States of America

2 3 4 5 6 7 8 9 10 09 08 07

Note to Educators and Parents

Reading is such an exciting adventure for young children! They are beginning to integrate their oral language skills with written language. To encourage children along the path to early literacy, books must be colorful, engaging, and interesting; they should invite the young reader to explore both the print and the pictures.

Animals I See at the Zoo is a new series designed to help children read about twelve fascinating animals. In each book, young readers will learn interesting facts about the featured animal.

Each book is specially designed to support the young reader in the reading process. The familiar topics are appealing to young children and invite them to read — and re-read — again and again. The full-color photographs and enhanced text further support the student during the reading process.

In addition to serving as wonderful picture books in schools, libraries, homes, and other places where children learn to love reading, these books are specifically intended to be read within an instructional guided reading group. This small group setting allows beginning readers to work with a fluent adult model as they make meaning from the text. After children develop fluency with the text and content, the book can be read independently. Children and adults alike will find these books supportive, engaging, and fun!

Una nota a los educadores y a los padres

¡La lectura es una emocionante aventura para los niños! En esta etapa están comenzando a integrar su manejo del lenguaje oral con el lenguaje escrito. Para fomentar la lectura desde una temprana edad, los libros deben ser vistosos, atractivos e interesantes; deben invitar al joven lector a explorar tanto el texto como las ilustraciones.

Animales que veo en el zoológico es una nueva serie pensada para ayudar a los niños a conocer cuatro animales fascinantes. En cada libro, los jóvenes lectores conocerán datos interesantes sobre ellos.

Cada libro ha sido especialmente diseñado para facilitar el proceso de lectura. La familiaridad con los temas tratados atrae la atención de los niños y los invita a leer — y releer — una y otra vez. Las fotografías a todo color y el tipo de letra facilitan aún más al estudiante el proceso de lectura.

Además de servir como fantásticos libros ilustrados en la escuela, la biblioteca, el hogar y otros lugares donde los niños aprenden a amar la lectura, estos libros han sido concebidos específicamente para ser leídos en grupos de instrucción guiada. Este contexto de grupos pequeños permite que los niños que se inician en la lectura trabajen con un adulto cuya fluidez les sirve de modelo para comprender el texto. Una vez que se han familiarizado con el texto y el contenido, los niños pueden leer los libros por su cuenta. ¡Tanto niños como adultos encontrarán que estos libros son útiles, entretenidos y divertidos!

— Susan Nations, M.Ed., author, literacy coach,
and consultant in literacy development

I like to go to the zoo.
I see bears at the zoo.

— — — — — — —

Me gusta ir al zoológico.
En el zoológico veo osos.

There are many kinds of bears. They live in many places. Black bears live in forests.

— — — — — — —

Hay muchos tipos de osos. Viven en muchos lugares. Los osos negros viven en el bosque.

Polar bears live where it is cold. Their thick fur helps keep them warm.

— — — — — — —

Los osos polares viven donde hace frío. La piel gruesa los ayuda a mantenerse calientes.

Their fur **blends** in with the snow. The animals they hunt cannot see them.

La piel **se mimetiza** con la nieve. Los animales que ellos cazan no los pueden ver.

Polar bears are good swimmers. They use their front paws to paddle.

— — — — — — —

Los osos polares son buenos nadadores. Usan las patas delanteras para remar.

Bears can stand on their hind legs. They sniff and look around for food.

- - - - - - -

Los osos pueden pararse en las patas traseras. Husmean y buscan comida.

All bears have sharp **claws**. They can use them to dig for food.

\- \- \- \- \- \- \- \-

Todos los osos tienen las **garras** afiladas. Pueden usarlas para escarbar y buscar comida.

claws/
garras

They can use them to **climb** trees. Bears are good at climbing.

– – – – – – – –

También pueden usar las garras para **treparse** a los árboles. Los osos son buenos para trepar.

I like to see bears
at the zoo. Do you?

▬ ▬ ▬ ▬ ▬ ▬ ▬

Me gusta ver los osos
en el zoológico.
¿Y a ti?

Glossary/Glosario

blends — mixes together so that the separate parts cannot be seen

mimetizarse — camuflarse para que no se distingan

claws — sharp, hooked nails on an animal's foot

garras — uñas afiladas y arqueadas en la pata de un animal

climb — to move up using the hands and feet

trepar — subir usando las manos y los pies

For More Information/Más información

Books/Libros

Macken, JoAnn Early. *Polar Animals. Animal Worlds* (series). Milwaukee: Gareth Stevens, 2002.

Sayre, April Pulley. *Splish! Splash! Animal Baths.* Brookfield, CT: The Millbrook Press, 2000.

Shahan, Sherry. *Feeding Time at the Zoo.* New York: Random House, 2000.

Web Sites/Páginas Web

NATIONALGEOGRAPHIC.COM

www.nationalgeographic.com/kids/creature_feature/0010/brownbears.html

www.nationalgeographic.com/kids/creature_feature/0011/pandas.html

www.nationalgeographic.com/kids/creature_feature/0004/polar.html

For fun facts, video, audio, maps, and postcards to send to your family and friends

Index/Índice

About the Author/Información sobre la autora

JoAnn Early Macken is the author of children's poetry, two rhyming picture books, *Cats on Judy* and *Sing-Along Song* and various other nonfiction series. She teaches children to write poetry and received the Barbara Juster Esbensen 2000 Poetry Teaching Award. JoAnn is a graduate of the MFA in Writing for Children Program at Vermont College. She lives in Wisconsin with her husband and their two sons.

JoAnn Early Macken es autora de poesía para niños. Ha escrito dos libros de rimas con ilustraciones, *Cats on Judy* y *Sing-Along Song* y otras series de libros educativos para niños. Ella enseña a los niños a escribir poesía y ha ganado el Premio Barbara Juster Esbensen en el año 2000. JoAnn se graduó con el título de "MFA" en el programa de escritura infantil de Vermont College. Vive en Wisconsin con su esposo y sus dos hijos.